DO YOU THINK GOD'S ARM IS TOO SHORT?

Things I Learned about God's Arm on My Life Journey
from Poverty to Richly Blessed Servant of God

KENNETH BOTTOMS, PhD

WESTBOW
P R E S S®
A DIVISION OF THOMAS NELSON
& ZONDERVAN

Scripture taken from the World English Bible.

WestBow Press books may be ordered through booksellers or by contacting:

WestBow Press
A Division of Thomas Nelson & Zondervan
1663 Liberty Drive
Bloomington, IN 47403
www.westbowpress.com
1 (866) 928-1240

Because of the dynamic nature of the Internet, any web addresses or links contained in this book may have changed since publication and may no longer be valid. The views expressed in this work are solely those of the author and do not necessarily reflect the views of the publisher, and the publisher hereby disclaims any responsibility for them.

Any people depicted in stock imagery provided by Getty Images are models, and such images are being used for illustrative purposes only. Certain stock imagery © Getty Images.

ISBN: 978-1-9736-2506-3 (sc)
ISBN: 978-1-9736-2508-7 (hc)
ISBN: 978-1-9736-2507-0 (e)

Library of Congress Control Number: 2018904177

Print information available on the last page.

WestBow Press rev. date: 4/20/2018

Dedicated to my Blessings Who Call me Papa

Brylie

Cooper

Peyton

Ella

INTRODUCTION

In Chapter 11 of the book of Numbers in the Old Testament, God tells Moses that He has heard the people constantly complaining about the manna he was providing them to eat. They wanted REAL MEAT to eat. So, God decided to provide them meat "until it is coming out their nostrils." Just prior to that, Moses told God that there is no way to come up with enough meat to feed that many people. If they slaughtered all their herds and flocks and caught all the fish in the sea, they wouldn't have enough. Moses was so frustrated that he was challenging God's power. Even after all the miracles that Moses had witnessed and experienced personally, he couldn't see any way to fulfill this latest demand from the people, so he explained to God how it was impossible to provide them with enough meat to meet their demands. God's response in Numbers 11:23: *"Is the Lord's arm too short?"* Or, in other words, "Do you think I don't have the power to do this little thing if I want to?" God created us and the world we live in. Let's not think there is some problem or issue that He can't handle. His arm is NOT too short! He can and will bless us beyond our wildest expectations if we open our eyes and allow Him to do so. I was born into poverty, but God's arm reached out to me all of my life (even when I wasn't aware of it) and blessed me in so many ways…spiritual, family, friends, career, financial prosperity, etc. … beyond my wildest dreams.

This book was written for my wonderful grandchildren who call me Papa. I hope and pray that they and others facing daily challenges will read it from time to time to find help, comfort, encouragement, counsel, and instruction from the Lord whose Arm is never too short, no matter what challenge they are facing.

THE BIBLE* SAYS:

For nothing is impossible with God. Luke 1:37

and

Listen to counsel and receive instruction that you may be wise in your latter end. Proverbs 19:20

All scriptures quoted in this book are from the World English Bible (WEB) translation.

CHAPTER 1

THE BEGINNING

When you were born, you cried and the world rejoiced. Live your life so that when your children think of fairness, caring, and integrity, they think of you.

– H. Jackson Brown, Jr., Author of Life's Little Instruction Book

Who am I, (Lord) Yahweh, and what is my house, that you have brought me thus far? 2 Samuel 7:18

I know how to be humbled, and I know how to abound. In everything and all things I have learned the secret both to be filled and to be hungry, both to abound and to be in need. Philippians 4:12

Where can I begin a book to testify that God's arm is not too short? Perhaps I should start at the beginning of my life on this earth to help you understand that it certainly took God's long arm to take me from my humble beginnings to where He has brought me so far.

In my current home, there is an old weathered sign hanging on the wall. It is a door hanger from the Kilgore Ice House. My mother, Emma Jo Jones, saved this old piece of cardboard for me as a keepsake from our first home where we lived with her parents (Jesse and Carrie Copeland) in a one-room house on N. Thompson Street in Kilgore, Texas.

Instead of a refrigerator, we had a wooden ice box at the small home there to keep food chilled. The "Ice Man" came down the street twice a week and checked the cardboard hanger pinned to the front screen door with a hair pin. He brought in a block of ice which weighed the number of pounds indicated by the orientation of the door hanger and placed it in the bottom of our "ice box."

Mother and her husband (Olen Bottoms) had been living there with her parents (a total of 4 adults!) in that one-room house before I was born, but he left soon after he learned she was pregnant with me. I was born in a charity hospital in Longview, Texas, and brought home to N. Thompson Street when we left the hospital.

We lived in this house for a couple of years until Mother re-married a wonderful man who became my beloved Dad (Oscar B. Jones). He met Mother after he returned from fighting in WW-II and learned that his wife had divorced him while he was overseas serving his country. He moved in with his brother and family who lived a block from where we were living on N. Thompson street. One of his first acts was to go down to the lumber yard, buy lumber, nails, and shingles on credit and build a small house nearby at 1105 Stone Street. It was close enough to the N. Thompson Street house that we shared the same outhouse. I grew up in that Stone Street house, and we lived there until I went away to college. It was hot in the summer (no air conditioning) and cold in the winter (heated by a single open-flame gas heater). There was no lock on the door, and it was not in a good part of town, but there was love in that home and God provided everything that we needed.

There is no way that I earned it or deserved it, but He continued to bless me throughout the remainder of my life. Of course, there were bumps in the road, hardships to endure, challenges to overcome, mistakes to be made, and many problems to handle with God's help. But somehow, even with that humble beginning on the earth, He got me through it all and blessed me with a great family, a sense of purpose, many opportunities to serve others, great financial success, and wonderful happiness. My purpose in writing this book is to share some of my "lessons learned" with my grandchildren. I hope and pray that it will help as they, and others who read this book, make important decisions along their life journey. If they discover, as I eventually did, that

God's arm is never too short, I am confident that they will have blessed lives!

▎REMEMBER:

- God's arm is not too short
- Keep this in mind as you face daily challenges

CHAPTER 2

BELIEVE IN GOD'S POWER

Challenges can be stepping stones or stumbling blocks. It just depends on how you view them.

– Author unknown

Trust in God with all your heart, and don't lean on your own understanding. In all your ways acknowledge him, and he will direct your paths. Proverbs 3:5-6

I am like a green olive tree in God's house. I trust in God's lovingkindness forever and ever. Psalms 52:8

"My grace is sufficient for you, for My power is made perfect in weakness." 2 Corinthians 12:9

My life has taken many twists and turns over the years since I was born in that charity hospital to a single unemployed mom ... but oh the blessings that I have received from God! At the time, as they were happening, I didn't always realize they were blessings.

- I had to earn enough money with odd jobs to pay for my school clothes starting in junior high.
- I had to work on dirty, dangerous oil rigs to earn enough money to go to college.
- I went into the military for four years during the Vietnam War.
- I lost my dad to a heart attack over 40 years ago, when I was a young man.
- I almost lost my son to a near death motorcycle accident when he was in college.
- I had to pull our kids out of school and away from their friends to move to another city due to job changes about every three or four years on average while they were growing up.
- I had to endure many tough and challenging jobs in my career.
- I had to live many years in cities where it gets very cold and snows a lot.
- I could go on and on with a list of things that seemed negative at the time but most were actually blessings that increased my faith and dependence on God.

Looking back, I can see the hand of God in all these things (except maybe the cold climates ... smile). He was continually preparing me for the next stage in my life. I had many setbacks, disappointments, and failures, but these are part of life in an imperfect world. God's power brought me through all of them and made me stronger.

I am an extreme introvert, but I had to overcome that on many occasions to succeed in my career. With God's help, I was able to do that. Let me give you an example of how my personality is very different from most people. A few years ago, I attended a group training meeting with about 30 of my peers, we all participated in an exercise to assess our personality types. At the end of the class, the leader wanted to point out that we all have different personalities, but many are similar, so he divided the classroom into 4 sections. We were each asked to move to the section of the room that aligned with our overall personality assessment. Three of the sections had about the same number of people in them. The fourth section only had one person in it, and that was me. I was an extreme introvert among a crowd of my peers who were much more extravertive. Most successful business leaders are extroverts with outgoing personalities. I can force myself to be outgoing and spend time with other people, but it drains my energy. I have to spend time alone to recharge my battery. It is interesting that my mother is just the opposite. She is very outgoing and is energized by being around people. She loves parties. I try to avoid parties. God made us all different, but I am amazed at what He has done with my life even with my introvertive personality. I truly feel like the olive tree in Psalms 52:8 quoted at the beginning of this chapter.

I also know that He and my guardian angel watch over me every moment of every day and they keep me from harm, whether I deserve that protection or not. My family will tell you that I am not a great driver. Some would say that I am a scary driver. I tend to think about other things while I am driving, and sometimes, driving makes me sleepy. I am reminded of the joke that no one wants to die in their sleep like grandpa because everyone else in the car when he died was screaming in terror. Nevertheless, God protects me while I am driving, while I am walking, and whatever I am doing. He also delivers solutions for dilemmas I face and gives me great clues to solutions for problems. He watches over me in small things as well as the big things. I am reminded of Psalms 23 ... **though I walk through the valley of the shadow of death ...**

A discussion of God's power would be incomplete without mentioning all of the evidence in nature. Look up into the heavens. Look at the ocean. Look at the mountains, deserts, hurricanes, tornados, earthquakes, floods, sunsets, rainbows, etc. God controls the universe, not just our little world, yet we need to look no farther than our own families to witness the miracle of birth, or our own back yard to see beautiful plants and flowers provided by God. He can do anything. His arm is not too short!

▌REMEMBER:

- Believe in God's power to help you, in spite of your weaknesses
- He has the power and He will protect you
- Observe His power in the world around you and in the blessings He gives you daily

CHAPTER 3

LISTEN

Listen to many. Speak to few.

— William Shakespeare

Courage is what it takes to stand up and speak. Courage is also what it takes to sit down and listen.

— Winston Churchill

Everyone should be quick to listen, slow to speak. James 1:19

Jesus answered, "It is written: 'Man shall not live on bread alone, but on every word that comes from the mouth of God.'" Matthew 4:4

Look to the Lord and His strength; seek His face always. Psalms 105:4

Early in life I found that I could learn more by listening than I could by talking. Perhaps that is just my personality to be a man of few words, but it has served me well over the years. I will admit that I have been criticized frequently because I don't talk much. However, that has never bothered me because I also have had the reputation of being someone who thinks before he speaks. Also, for some reason when I do speak, people tend to listen to what I say. Everybody is different. Nobody is perfect, certainly not me. But that approach has worked for me. Most people enjoy frequent verbal communications, and that is fine. Speak a lot or a little based on your individual gifts, but I recommend that you also make sure you listen.

I understand that listening also worked for President Dwight Eisenhower, who was also the great American 5-star general who led us and our European allies to victory in World War II. He said, "Never miss an opportunity to keep your mouth shut." He was a great listener and leader.

However, the most important part of listening is to decide what is worth hearing and try to avoid the rest as best you can. We are flooded from all sides with media noise, inaccurate information, false advertising, misdirection of all sorts, etc. My advice is to choose carefully what enters your brain. As they say, "garbage in means garbage comes out." If we allow too much bad stuff into our brain, it is hard for our brain to produce useful outputs. I recommend that you read good books, watch good videos/programs on your electronic devices, spend time with good people who can help you grow and learn, read your Bible every day, and observe your surroundings wherever you are. Be on the lookout for messages from God.

In addition to expanding your knowledge, a habit of good listening/observation also helps you be more attuned to the needs of other people ... your friends, your family, your neighbors. Listening and observing helps you avoid being internally focused and helps you identify things you can do to help other people.

Above all else, listen to God. He is constantly sending us blessings and messages. So often, we miss them because we are not listening for them. Look for these messages and listen to what He is communicating to you. I see God's hand in so many ways every day. Sometimes, it's something small like providing an opening in traffic so I can safely change lanes. Sometimes he takes me on an unplanned route to get me to see something. Sometimes it's larger, like when he had me serve four years in the Air Force during the Vietnam War. I was in the prime of my life and felt like the four years I spent in the military put me far behind my peers in the business world who found a way to avoid military service. For decades, I thought there was absolutely no reason for God to take me away from my career for such a long time. Then I started doing volunteer work to help others and found that I could help other veterans much more effectively since I was a veteran myself. I knew what it was like to wear the uniform and sacrifice for my country just as they did. My long years in the Air Force were not wasted. I was put there for the sole purpose of preparing me to help others. It took me decades to hear this message from God. Grandchildren and others who read this book: I hope you do a better job of listening to God than I did in my younger years. God's arm is not too short!

REMEMBER:

- Listen to God for important messages.

CHAPTER 4

TALK TO GOD

Prayer is the key of the morning and the bolt of the evening.

— Mahatma Gandhi

To be a Christian without prayer is no more possible than to be alive without breathing.

— Martin Luther

I believe that prayer is our powerful contact with the greatest force in the universe.

— Actress Loretta Young

Pray without ceasing. In everything give thanks, for this is the will of God in Christ Jesus toward you. 1 Thessalonians 5:17-18

Continue steadfastly in prayer Colossians 4:2

Believe before you receive. *Therefore, I tell you, all things whatever you pray and ask for, believe that you receive them, and you shall have them. Mark 11: 24*

But I tell you, love your enemies, bless those who curse you, do good to those who hate you, and pray for those who spitefully use you and persecute you. Matthew 5:44

There is a country song where an old man is asked how he was able to have a long, successful, happy life and, among other things, he says "Don't let your prayin' knees get lazy and love like crazy." What a great statement on prayer. When I was growing up, the men at the small church we attended would get down on one knee and bow their heads during prayer. The women remained in their pew. I never really heard the reason. I suppose it was because they were wearing dresses and nylon stockings (no pants allowed in church in those days), and it would have been awkward for them to do what the men were doing. Bowing or kneeling is a symbol of humility before God. Getting down on your knees is not necessary but talking to God is necessary. You can pray any time from any position but pray you must.

Jesus' disciples asked Him to teach them to pray. Here is how he responded:

"Pray like this:

> *'Our Father Who is in heaven, may Your name be kept holy.*
> *May Your kingdom come.*
> *May Your will be done, as in heaven, so on earth.*
> *Give us this day our daily bread.*
> *Forgive us our debts, as we also forgive our debtors.*
> *Bring us not into temptation but deliver us from evil.*
> *For Yours is the kingdom, the power and the glory forever. Amen.'" Matthew 6:9-13*

Whether you realize it or not, God is alive and active in your life. He sent the Bible to speak to us and He sends us messages through miracles (small and great) that He performs for us every day. We just don't always have our eyes open to what He is doing for us. But He doesn't want this to be a one-way conversation with Him being the only one doing the communicating. He wants it to be two-way, and that's where prayer comes in. As He said in 1 Thessalonians, we should pray without ceasing and give thanks for everything. Let Him know what you need. He already knows, but He wants to hear it from you. Also, believe that you will get what you are asking for and you will get it. God has long arms.

▌REMEMBER:

- Don't let your praying knees get lazy
- Pray without ceasing
- Believe first and you will receive

CHAPTER 5

CHOOSE YOUR FRIENDS CAREFULLY

Be careful the environment you choose for it will shape you; be careful the friends you choose for you will become like them.

– W. Clement Stone

Life is partly what we make it, and partly what it is made by the friends we choose.

– Tennessee Williams

You choose your friends by their character and your socks by their color.

– Gary Oldman

The righteous choose their friends carefully, but the way of the wicked leads them astray.
Proverbs 12:26

A man of many companions may be ruined, but there is a friend who sticks closer than a brother. Proverbs 18:24

The second time we lived in St Louis, we had the good fortune of getting to know Gene Stallings and his family. We attended church together and we welcomed them into our home for dinner. We also had dinner in their home. Gene was (and still is) a celebrity. At the time, he was head coach of the NFL football team in St Louis, the St Louis Cardinals. This was before he and the team moved to Arizona to become the Arizona Cardinals. He later left the NFL to re-establish a football powerhouse at his alma mater, the University of Alabama ... taking them to a national championship before he retired. Even our teenage children listened when a man of Gene's stature spoke to them. The advice that he always gave our kids and other kids every time he talked to them was: "Choose your friends carefully." I think that is such great wisdom from a man who coached college kids and professional athletes all of his life. He knew how kids (and adults) can get in with the wrong crowd and ruin their lives, or on the other hand they can develop good friends who can help them become successful in life.

The scriptures are filled with examples of important friendships such as David and his friend Jonathan who saved David's life when Jonathan's father, King Saul, was trying to kill David. The word "friends" is used over 100 times in the Bible. God wants us to have good friends like Jonathan, but He also recognizes that we don't need friends like Job had in the book of Job. Job's friends tried to get him to turn away from God when disaster hit his life. Job continued to believe that God had a long arm. After losing all that he had, including his health, he was blessed with even more wealth and blessings than he had before.

Friends have had a positive influence on me throughout my life. I have never had many close friends because, as an introvert, I tend to be a loner. Nevertheless, friends have helped me to:

- Survive high school even though I was an introvert and came from a poor family
- Choose a college degree program
- Decide to go to a college where I eventually met my beautiful and wonderful wife
- Grow spiritually
- Depend on God and his long arm
- Rear truly wonderful children who blessed us by choosing great spouses and giving us outstanding grandchildren
- Become financially independent with God's help
- Provide moral and on-the-ground support for my aged mother while I was living in another state
- And many other things too numerous to list here.

I have also been blessed never to get in with "the wrong crowd" of friends who would lead me astray. I see God's long arm at work there too …

▌REMEMBER:

- The wisest man who ever lived (Solomon), said in the book of Proverbs and Gene Stallings frequently told my young children and many other teens: **"CHOOSE YOUR FRIENDS CAREFULLY."**

- The right friends will provide a positive influence on your life; the wrong friends will lead you down the path to misery and hardship in the end.

CHAPTER 6

DO THE RIGHT THING FOR YOUR FAMILY

I believe in the value of life. I believe we must prepare our children for tomorrow with the family values of my grandparents.

– Ryan Zinke, Congressman

The lessons I learned from my mother and her friends have guided me through death, birth, loss, love, failure, and achievement, on to a Fulbright scholarship and Harvard Business School. They taught me to believe that anything was possible. They have proven to be the strongest family values I could ever have imagined.

– Gayle Tzemach Lemmon, best-selling author and journalist

Whoever brings ruin on their family will inherit the wind. Proverbs 11:29

Peace be within your walls. Psalms 122:7

Train up a child in the way he should go, and when he is old, he will not depart from it. Proverbs 22:6

God gave us families for a reason. They are intended to provide loving companionship and a safe, nurturing environment for the rearing of children.

It all starts with selecting the right spouse. This is unbelievably important. Your spouse can make you happy or miserable for the rest of your life. I say rest of your life because it is a lifetime commitment. Divorces were allowed in the Old Testament, but Jesus put an end to that when He came. In Matthew 19:9, He said "I tell you that whoever divorces his wife, except for sexual immorality, and will marry another, commits adultery; and he who marries her when she is divorced commits adultery."

Take time to get to know your future spouse … not sexually … that is sinning against God, and you will be blessed beyond belief if you wait on that until you are married. But get to know their values and beliefs and how they think … what is important to them. Make sure you are compatible and can make each other happy. You will also need to get to know their family. The old saying is true that you marry your spouse's family as well as your spouse. You will be spending a lot of time with that family after you are married, and don't forget that your spouse's parents will be grandparents to your children.

I want to make a request to each of my grandchildren. I ask that … before you commit to marrying someone … please do three things:

1. Pray about it.

2. Get your parents' approval. You guys are the luckiest children in the world. You won the birth lottery when God blessed you with such outstanding parents. They know you better than anyone else and they will always want what is best for you.

3. Read this short book again. Is this someone who shares your values, beliefs, and will be your lifelong spiritual partner?

I am an old man, and I may not be alive when you make that decision, but I will be happy to give you my input if I am still here (Grandma will be willing to do that too!). If I am gone, you should know that I will be watching over you from heaven and God will be too. When you read this little book again, please pay particular attention to this chapter. Make sure you are going to marry someone who loves God as much as you do. I cannot emphasize enough that this is one of the most important choices you will make in your whole life. Your future happiness depends on it.

Happy wife-happy life. This is an old saying and the corollary is also true for wives: Happy husband-happy life. If your spouse is happy, it will dramatically improve the quality of your life. Dr. Laura Schlesinger is a certified Family and Marriage Counselor who has a popular radio show in which she provides practical advice to callers with marriage or family issues. She has also written several books on this topic. I really like the advice she gives to her callers, especially the following which I am paraphrasing based on my memory of advice I heard her give on her radio show so many times:

1. Don't marry too young. Our mind is still developing and changing at least through our mid-20s, and perhaps beyond that age.
2. Date a minimum of 2 years before marriage. Get to know if you are compatible with this person, but don't ever move in ("shack up") with them before marriage.
3. After you marry, wake up in the morning and look at your spouse and think about what you can do today to make them happy they are alive and married to you.
4. If the subject of divorce comes up, work things out unless your spouse is physically abusive.
5. If you divorce (for any reason), no re-marriage or dating until your kids are grown and out of the house. Bringing another adult into the house is tough on children and will create problems for them both now and later.
6. She concludes each segment of her radio show with "Now go do the right thing."

Marriage is a commitment made in heaven that lasts until death. There will be many ups and downs over the years. It will take hard work by both spouses to make it work right, but it can be done, and should be done for you to enjoy the happiness that God intended. Marriages encounter sickness and health, better times and worse times, disagreements and arguments, financial issues, etc. It will not be all smooth sailing. There will be tough times but you can make it work and even make it thrive. It is up to you and your spouse to work it out. It is worth the effort. It won't be easy, but

"Do the right thing." Think about 1 Corinthians 13, the chapter on love. In verse 7, it says that love *"bears all things, believes all things, hopes all things, endures all things."*

Grandma (the former Anne Kelley) and I got married only a couple of days after I graduated from Officer Training School and received my commission to become an Air Force officer. Immediately after a brief and low-cost honeymoon in San Antonio, Texas, I had to report to my first duty station in Oklahoma. We loaded my small car with our very modest amount of possessions and found a little apartment in Oklahoma City not far from the Air Force base where I was stationed. My mother-in-law was concerned about how we would handle arguments and conflicts because she knew her daughter had a temper. So, she asked your Grandma if we were fighting yet, and wondered how it was going. Grandma told her that I refused to fight or argue. Instead, I left the apartment and went outside to work on our car. She told her mom that we had the best tuned car in Oklahoma ... and we had no fights or arguments. It takes two sides to argue and fight.

Many years later, we were living in New Jersey in a house with a finished basement. At a model home in our neighborhood, I saw that they had removed the door at the entrance to the finished basement and it changed the feel of that area. It appeared that the basement wasn't a basement at all, but it was just another floor in the house that was down one level. I liked that idea and told Grandma that we should do that. She disagreed. We "discussed" it and I told her my rationale for the change. She had not had a chance to think about it in advance like I had. I am an engineer by training and try to think things through before coming to a logical conclusion. She decided she couldn't win the argument even though she disagreed with it, so she said I should just take off "THE DOOR." We don't use profanity and seldom raise our voices in our house or elsewhere, but we do occasionally look back with humor at "THE DOOR" incident. At least, I think we look back on it with humor. I certainly do, but maybe not so much in her mind. Nevertheless, now I try to get her involved earlier in decisions, so that it doesn't look like I have already made up my mind before I bring up a topic. By the way, we removed "THE DOOR" and it looked great!

▌REMEMBER:

- Marriage is a lifetime commitment.
- Both people in the marriage have to work hard to make it a success.
- Happy wife (or husband) means happy life.

CHAPTER 7

WORK HARD

The harder you work, the luckier you get.

– Gary Player,
Hall of Fame Professional Golfer

Mohammed Ali, perhaps the greatest boxer who ever lived, said, "I hated every minute of training but I said, 'Don't quit. Suffer now and live the rest of your life as a champion.'"

And whatever you do, <u>work heartily, as for the Lord, and not for men</u>. Colossians 3:23

But seek first God's Kingdom and his righteousness; and all these things will be added to you. Matthew 6:33

... <u>let him labor, producing with his hands something that is good, that he may have something to give to him who has need</u>. Ephesians 4:28

... make it your ambition to lead a quiet life, and to do your own business, and to <u>work with your own hands</u>, even as we instructed you; that you may walk properly toward those who are outside <u>and that you may have need of nothing</u>. 1 Thessalonians 4:10-12

I grew up in a godly family of hard workers. Life was hard for my parents, but they worked tirelessly to make sure we had our basic needs met. They also encouraged me to work. As a pre-teen, I mowed yards and found other odd jobs to earn spending money. When I made it to Junior High, I walked over two miles each way to the country club and started working as a caddy. I earned 90 cents (plus maybe a tip of 10 cents) for carrying a golf bag 18 holes (about 4 or 5 hours) and then worked in the golf shop cleaning golf clubs until after dark. I was paid for the club cleaning in candy instead of money, but that was ok. I made enough each summer to buy my own school clothes every year.

In High School, I worked in the country club pro shop and had other jobs around the golf course. When I was a senior, my step-dad had a heart attack and couldn't work for a long time. Mother went to work in the junior college cafeteria because Dad didn't get paid when he couldn't work. Even when he was working, there was no money for me to go to college, but my parents insisted that I get a college education and break the cycle of low income in our family. I worked in the oilfield as a roughneck and roustabout to pay all of my college expenses and pay cash for a used Ford Falcon to get back and forth to college. The oilfield paid a lot better than my caddy job ($1.45 per hour in the oilfield) but it was hard, dirty and dangerous work. This was in the late 1960s before the government established safety regulations. My cousin who lived across the street from us lost an arm working in the oilfield. One of the men that I worked with was cut half in two at the waist. Many lost fingers and toes, but God watched out for me as He always did. I was knocked off the drilling rig platform once but landed on my back on a rack of pipe 10 feet below and only had the wind knocked out of me. During the summer, the normal hours (7 days a week most of the time) were 12-hour shifts, not including travel time to and from the rigs, which was usually an hour each way. So, here is what my schedule looked like every day:

- I got up at 3:30 am to dress, eat breakfast, and get to the company's work yard by 4:30 am
- Rode in the company car from the work yard with other members of the crew to the site of the oil rig
- Arrived at the rig site by 5:30am to relieve the night crew
- Worked 12-hour shift until 5:30pm
- Returned to the company work yard around 6:30pm
- Drove home and arrived by 7:00pm
- Took a shower, ate dinner and went to bed by 8:30pm so I could be up at 3:30am the next morning to do it again.

I filled in for other oilfield hands during Christmas vacation to earn spending money. I still remember the last day that I did that. The weather forecast was for the temperature to drop down into the teens, and a lot of the oilfield workers called in sick. A college buddy and I were called to fill in on the night shift (5:30pm to 5:30am). It was REALLY COLD and we had to pull a "wet string." What that means is that we had to pull all of the tubing (pipes in the center part of the well) out of the well, disconnect them, and tie them back on the side of the platform. Most of the time, there is no water or oil in the pipes as they come out of the ground, but on this particular night, there was water in the pipes. As a result, those of us on the platform disconnecting each pipe got drenched with it every time we disconnected a pipe. We were miserable as the water froze on our clothes. No wonder so many of the crew had called in sick that night! That was my last time to work in the oilfield. It provided great motivation to go back to college in the fall and finish my degree.

Other than Christmas Break, Spring Break, and the summer holiday, I didn't try to work at a job while I was going to Texas Tech. I focused on my electrical engineering classes which didn't leave time for employment while I was taking classes. My job in college was to earn a degree and make good grades. This often required a lot of "all-nighters" for studying and I had very little time for socializing. Shortly after graduation, I joined the Air Force and married my college sweetheart, but the work ethic that I learned early in life continued with me throughout the many years of my career in the business world. In fact, I often worked too much when the kids were little. On weekdays, they were asleep when I left for work and were awake only a few hours in the evening after I got home from work. So, I volunteered to be the one who got up with them during the night if they needed a diaper change, a soothing voice, a drink of water, etc. I still love being a dad, even though they are now successful and thriving adults with their own children, and don't need me in the middle of the night anymore.

Every man also to whom God has given riches and wealth, and has given him power to eat of it, and to take his

portion, and <u>to rejoice in his labor – this is the gift of God</u>. **Ecclesiastes 5:19**

▎REMEMBER:

- Work hard and do your best, as if God is your boss, not someone at the company where you work.
- Rejoice in your labor.

CHAPTER 8

BE BOLD

"Behold the turtle. He makes progress only when he sticks his neck out."

– James Bryant Conant, famous chemist and President of Harvard University 1933-1953

For God didn't give us a spirit of fear, but of power and love and discipline. 2 Timothy 1:7

If God is for us, who can be against us? Romans 8:31

Therefore since we have such a hope, <u>we are very bold</u>. 2 Corinthians 3:12

Only be strong and very courageous, to observe to do according to all the law, which Moses my servant commanded you. Don't turn from it to the right hand or to the left, that you may have good success wherever you go. Joshua 1:7

Let's therefore draw near with boldness to the throne of grace, that we may receive mercy and may find grace for help in time of need. Hebrews 4:16

There is a song from a few years ago called "I Hope You Dance." The message of the song is a great one. It encourages the listener to step out and take advantage of opportunities as they come along. If you get a chance to do something worthwhile, don't sit on the sidelines. Get involved. Be bold.

As I mentioned in another chapter, I tend to be analytical and think through an issue or an opportunity before making a decision. That is ok unless you let an opportunity pass you by as you stand on the sidelines thinking about it. There are some opportunities that you should just pass up, but many that you should not. Ask God to help you with the decisions and let Him lead you to the opportunity. Don't be afraid to be bold and step out in faith. God will lead you through it regardless of the outcome ... success or failure. Failures are just more learning and growth opportunities. I can testify to that because I have survived many failures and setbacks.

Also, as I mentioned earlier, I am an introvert ... not just sort of introvertive. I am an INTROVERT. It has always been a challenge for me to force myself to act boldly. I hate to draw attention to myself. Nevertheless, with God's help, I have stepped out and taken risks to go where He has led me. My career is a good example.

I have relocated my family across the country numerous times to advance my career, but one of the most memorable bold moves was the one that took us from San Antonio, Texas to Philadelphia, Pennsylvania. I have always loved San Antonio. It is probably my favorite city in the world. I was working for AT&T in St Louis, Missouri when the corporate headquarters was moved from St Louis to San Antonio. Since I worked in the corporate office, I was thrilled with that move. However, after only a year in San Antonio, I was passed over for a promotion and had to train the man who did get the promotion. That was God's way of telling me that I was not going to stay in San Antonio, but I didn't recognize it at the time. The bottom line is that I received a job offer to leave AT&T for a large insurance company headquartered in Philadelphia. Keep in mind that I am a native Texan, now living in the city of my dreams, albeit having to train the guy who got the job I had been promised. Moving to the East coast seemed like a really bad idea, but God kept pushing. AT&T offered a voluntary early retirement package to all managers, and CIGNA Insurance Company in Philadelphia offered me a compensation package that was hard to pass up. I told my friends that I considered a move from Texas to the northeast to be an international move. It was like moving to another country, not just to another state. Things were rocky there at first. The job was not what I thought it would be, the weather was so cold, the culture was so different, and we were so far from our family back in Texas. Nevertheless, it became the best career move I ever made. I made treasured lifelong friends there and became truly successful financially. When I was promoted to an executive position there, I told my mother who did not like her job to retire and I would send her a check every month. I have been doing that now for over 20 years. It turns out that God's arm is not too short. He can move a poor Texas boy across the country to a difficult environment and give him success beyond his dreams. I still can't understand why I was the one who received such great blessings.

▌REMEMBER:

- God gave us a spirit of power ... not fear.
- Be bold. God's arm will be there for you.

CHAPTER 9

BE PATIENT

Patience, persistence and perspiration make an unbeatable combination for success.

– Napoleon Hill

Patience is bitter but its fruit is sweet.

– Jean-Jacques Rousseau

Have patience. All things are difficult before they become easy.

– Saadi

Rest in Yahweh (God), and wait patiently for him. Psalms 37:7

Even the youths shall faint and be weary, and the young men shall utterly fall: but those who wait for Yahweh (God) shall renew their strength; they shall mount up with wings as eagles; they shall run, and not be weary; they shall walk, and not faint. Isaiah 40:30-31

But don't forget this one thing, beloved, that one day is with the Lord as a thousand years, and a thousand years as one day. The Lord is not slow concerning His promise, as some count slowness. 2 Peter 3:8-9

We live in an impatient world. We want everything to happen immediately. Fast food restaurants are everywhere. When we turn on a light switch, we expect immediate light. When we turn on our phone, tv, or any other electronic device, we expect them to come on immediately. Waiting is a lost art.

The important thing to remember in life is that we need to be patient and wait on the Lord. His timing is different from ours. He can see the future and know that everything will turn out alright. We don't have that power, so we get impatient.

After Anne and I had been married for a couple of years, we decided we wanted to have children. However, we kept trying and it appeared that it was not going to be possible. We were not patient. We didn't wait on God's timing. Instead, we decided to take matters into our own hands and adopt a child. We were living in Oklahoma and they, like most states, have a long process for pre-approval of adoptive parents. It includes interviews by social workers, taking classes, and learning about being a parent. We went through most of the process and were excited that we were on the threshold of finally becoming parents when we learned that Anne was pregnant. Obviously, we were thrilled, but, looking back, I can see how God was in charge and we had to go with His timing instead of ours. Our feeble attempt to accelerate the process didn't work. God was the one who decided when our first child would be born, not us. It reminded me of the story of Abraham and Sarah. They didn't think that Sarah would ever have a child and decided to fix it on their own instead of waiting for God. They found a way for Abraham to become a father through Sarah's handmaid servant, but that caused them all sorts of problems. In the end, Sarah became pregnant in her old age and her son Isaac was born. He became the next generation of the Jewish nation that brought Christ into the world.

I can think of many cases in my life where I was not patient and things didn't work out quite like I wanted. However, I can also think of many cases where patience paid off and I received a better outcome by waiting on the Lord instead of trying to force the timing that I wanted. There is such peace in turning the timing over to God instead of trying to come up with a way to address the issue some other way.

Wise King Solomon wrote in Ecclesiastes chapter 3:

1. For everything there is a season, and a time for every purpose under heaven:
2. A time to be born, and a time to die; a time to plant, and a time to pluck up that which is planted;
3. A time to kill, and a time to heal; a time to break down, and a time to build up;
4. A time to weep, and a time to laugh; a time to mourn, and a time to dance;
5. A time to cast away stones, and a time to gather stones together; a time to embrace, and a time to refrain from embracing;
6. A time to seek, and a time to lose; a time to keep, and a time to cast away;
7. A time to tear, and a time to sew; a time to keep silence, and a time to speak;

8. A time to love, and a time to hate; a time for war, and a time for peace.

▌REMEMBER:

- Depend on God for the timing.
- Waiting on the Lord (patience) will be rewarded in the end.

CHAPTER 10

DON'T WORRY - BE HAPPY

Happiness is a choice. You can choose to be happy. There's going to be stress in life, but it's your choice whether you let it affect you or not.

— Valerie Bertinelli

Most people are about as happy as they make up their minds to be.

— Abraham Lincoln

Happiness is an inside job.

— Author unknown

No one can make you feel inferior without your consent.

— First Lady Eleanor Roosevelt

THE BIBLE SAYS:

I know that <u>there is nothing better for them than to rejoice [or be happy]</u> and do good as long as they live. Ecclesiastes 3:12

Yet I am not alone, because the Father is with me. I have told you these things, that in me you may have peace. <u>In the world you have trouble; but cheer up!</u> I have overcome the world. John 16:32-33

Jesus said: "Who of you by worrying can add a single hour to your life? Since you cannot do this very little thing, why do you worry about the rest?" Luke 12:25-26

In nothing be anxious but in everything, by prayer and petition with thanksgiving, let your requests be made known to God. And the peace of God, which surpasses all understanding, will guard your hearts and your thoughts in Christ Jesus. Philippians 4:6-7

In some versions of the Bible, the words "to rejoice" are translated "be happy" in the above quote from Ecclesiastes. Thus, Solomon, the author of Ecclesiastes and the wisest person to ever live, is saying that there is nothing better than to be happy and do good as long as you live. I love that!

Many years ago, when I was doing post-graduate studies at Washington University in St Louis, Missouri, I had a great professor who opened my eyes to happiness and peace of mind. I tried to get my company to hire him to enlighten our employees and help them learn the secret to taking charge of your emotions, but there was no money in the budget. What a shame, but I tried to spread the word whenever I had the chance. Here is the bottom line of what he taught me:

- Happiness is a choice that you make for yourself.
- No one else can make you happy or unhappy unless you turn over control of your emotions to them.

One of the examples he gave was road rage. If you are driving and someone cuts you off or almost causes you to be in an accident, the normal reaction is to become angry at that person for doing that to you. You might say something like, "He made me mad!" but my professor would say that you chose to be mad. His point was that you can choose to be angry or choose not to be angry. You can choose to be happy in any situation if you want to do so. If you turn over control of your emotions to others, they can make you happy or angry or sad or whatever. But if you retain control and make those decisions yourself, you can be happy in any situation. Admittedly, it takes some practice and discipline to learn the necessary self-control. Nevertheless, happiness is a choice that you make for yourself. It should not be something that others can steal from you unless you allow them to do so.

My mother is an awesome example of choosing to be happy. She married young, was deserted by her first husband when he found out she was pregnant, lived many years on the bottom rung of society, lost her parents while I was still a child, lost her second husband to a heart attack when she was 50 years old, lost my brother to cancer when he was age 44 (and she was 66), was a robbery victim at home and at work, and suffered numerous other tragedies throughout her life. She has every right to be a bitter old woman, but she has always been (and continues to be at age 92) just the opposite. She is a happy person dependent on God. She laughs a lot and enjoys life. Everyone loves her because of her cheerful attitude which is contagious.

Life is filled with choices. We make them every day. Someone once told me that the choices you make today create the story you tell about your life tomorrow. That just means that our daily choices create the record of our life on earth. After all of the choices have been made, we look back at the story of a life well lived or one that was wasted. Someone else told me once that we create our own future by the choices we make. That is also true. Decisions made today will affect your life not just today, but it will also affect your tomorrows.

Whether we think of our choices as creating the story of our life or as creating our own future, both thoughts capture the immense impact of our choices. Solomon's wisdom was from God and his words in Ecclesiastes (see quote above) was great advice:

- Be happy
- Do good

Jesus followed that up in the New Testament with:

- Don't worry

I hope you will choose to be happy and choose not to worry. Don't let others make choices for you. You can make the right choices with the help of God's long arm.

As long as you live, keep smiling because it brightens everybody's day. Vin Scully, famous sportscaster

▌REMEMBER:

- Choose to be happy.
- Choose to do good.
- Choose not to worry.
- Make your own decisions. Don't let others control your emotions.

CHAPTER 11

REMEMBER THAT LIFE IS NOT FAIR (NO WHINING)

Life is never fair, and perhaps it is a good thing for most of us that it is not.

– Oscar Wilde

We have to acknowledge that adolescence is that time of transition where we begin to introduce to children that life isn't pretty, that there are difficult things, there are hard situations, it's not fair. Bad things happen to good people.

– Laurie Halse Anderson

For He makes His sun to rise on the evil and the good and sends rain on the just and unjust. Matthew 5:45

I was envious of the arrogant, when I saw the prosperity of the wicked. Psalms 73:3

For our light and momentary troubles are achieving for us an eternal glory that far outweighs them all. 2 Corinthians 4:17

As you go through life, it becomes obvious that life is not always fair. Bad things happen to good people and good things happen to bad people. Don't let that be a distraction for you. In an earlier chapter, I mentioned a number of things that happened during my life that I didn't like at the time but they turned out to be blessings. I like to think of many of them as if they were grains of sand and I was an oyster. When an unwanted grain of sand somehow gets inside an oyster, it irritates the oyster but it eventually turns into a pearl as the oyster deals with it. The thing the oyster didn't want, but had to deal with anyway, turned into something of great value.

Also, don't compare yourself with others or be envious of others. For one thing, you don't really know their story or how they really feel inside. You might look at someone who is very wealthy and think they are happy, but frequently that is not really the case. King Solomon in the Old Testament was the wisest man who ever lived. He was also probably one of the richest and most powerful men who has ever lived. Yet, at the end of his life, he was not happy. He started out putting God first, but somewhere along the way, he was distracted by things of this world and lost his focus on God. So sad.

Remember something important. You don't know what will happen in your life until after you have lived it. While you are on the journey through the years, there will be pain and suffering as well as victories and celebrations, successes and failures. Enjoy the journey, including the ups and downs. Put yourself in God's hands throughout your life and everything will be fine. No whining. God's arm is long enough to get you through anything that comes along.

When things are not going well, go to God's word for comfort. I especially like the following words from Psalms 23:

1. *The Lord is my shepherd: I shall lack nothing.*
2. *He makes me to lie down in green pastures. He leads me beside still waters.*
3. *He restores my soul. He guides me in the paths of righteousness for His name's sake.*
4. *Even though I walk through the valley of the shadow of death, I will fear no evil, for You are with me. Your rod and your staff, they comfort me.*
5. *You prepare a table before me in the presence of my enemies. You have anointed my head with oil. My cup runs over.*
6. *Surely goodness and mercy shall follow me all the days of my life, and I shall dwell in God's house forever.*

▎REMEMBER:

- Life is not fair.
- Overcoming great obstacles can result in great achievements with the help of God's arm.
- Enjoy your journey through life as you put yourself in God's hands.

CHAPTER 12

REMEMBER THE GOLDEN RULE

My philosophy is to do the best you can for somebody. Help. It's how you treat people decently. There isn't anything better than the golden rule. It's in every major religion in one language or another.

– Art Linkletter

"Be kind for everyone you meet is fighting a hard battle."

– Author Unknown

When asked which of the commandments is the most important, Jesus answered, "The greatest is, 'Hear, Israel, the Lord our God, the Lord is one: you shall love the Lord your God with all your heart, and with all your soul, and with all your mind, and with all your strength.' This is the first commandment. The second is like this, 'You shall love your neighbor as yourself.' There is no other commandment greater than these." - Mark 12:29-31

Jesus's second command is often also interpreted as the Golden Rule which is "Do unto others as you would have them do unto you." That is another way of making the statement, and it helps us understand what he was saying about loving your neighbor as yourself.

When I was growing up, I often heard another old saying. It was attributed to American Indians and said that "You should not judge a man until you have walked in his moccasins for at least a mile." Everyone has problems or issues they are dealing with and it usually affects how they act and what they do. Instead of being quick to judge or criticize, think about how you can do an act of kindness and perhaps make someone's day a little brighter. Remember that Jesus said that we should even love our enemies.

Over the years, I have lived and visited in big cities with various types of beggars on the street. In my younger days, I often tended to look down on these people as addicts or lazy people who were unwilling to straighten up their lives and earn a living on their own. As I matured, I changed my attitude. Stuff happens, and often it seems beyond our control … Loss of a job, illness, divorce, physical/mental handicap, etc. I decided that I don't know the situation of these people and I started giving beggars a few bucks or buying them a meal. A friend once told me that the beggar we just passed would use the money I gave him to buy alcohol or drugs. I told my friend that I don't know that beggar's situation and he is the one who will have to answer to God if he lied to me about needing the money to purchase food. I did what I could to love my neighbor and let God be the judge.

One time when our children were in their pre-teen years, we drove to Corpus Christi, Texas on vacation. We stopped along the way and I left my family in the car while I went into a convenience store. I had to purchase some snacks and ice that we would be needing when we reached our destination. A woman was standing by the front door of the store and she told me she was homeless and needed food for her family. I put myself in her shoes and bought her a couple of bags of groceries, which is what I hope someone would have done for me if I had been in that situation. When I returned to the car, my children asked about the woman and I just told them that she was homeless and needed help. I didn't think any more about it, but many years later, my children reminded me about the time we helped the lady on the way to Corpus Christi. I had no idea that small act of kindness would stick in their minds all those years. I had forgotten all about it, but in addition to helping that lady and her family, it turned out that my children learned how to treat others in need. To this day, they continue to reach out to others who are less fortunate and in need of help. They make me so proud!

Volunteering to help incarcerated veterans in state and federal penitentiaries as well as helping children in the Texas state foster care system has provided me frequent opportunities to practice the Golden Rule. Many veterans are in prison only because serving in the military warped their mind, and they got into serious trouble as a result. Others deserve to be there, but they are all my brothers and need to be helped.

Many children, through no fault of their own, end up in tragic circumstances and need help. I approach each situation prayerfully with the attitude that but for the grace of God, I could have been incarcerated or my children could have been swept up in the foster care system. I try to help these veterans and foster children like I would like to be helped if I were in their situation.

▌REMEMBER:

- The golden rule: Love your neighbor as yourself.
- Everyone is your neighbor (even those you don't like).

CHAPTER 13

BE GENEROUS

Remember that the happiest people are not those getting more, but those giving more.

– H. Jackson Brown, Jr.

True generosity is an offering; given freely and out of pure love. No strings attached. No expectations. Time and love are the most valuable possessions you can share.

– Suze Orman

To practice five things under all circumstances constitutes perfect virtue; these five are gravity, generosity of soul, sincerity, earnestness, and kindness.

– Confucius

Let each give according as he has determined in his heart; not grudgingly, or under compulsion; for God loves a cheerful giver. 2 Corinthians 9:7

"Will a man rob God? ... Bring the whole tithe into the storehouse ... and test me now in this," says Yahweh (God) of hosts, "if I will not open you the windows (floodgates) of heaven, and pour you out a blessing, that there shall not be room enough for." Malachi 3:8, 10

For they all gave out of their abundance, but she, out of her poverty, gave all that she had to live on. Mark 12:44

In the Old Testament, God required tithing, which means giving 10% of your income. We are no longer under the Old Testament (the Law of Moses), but Jesus said that law was given to teach us about God. We are under a new law of grace that was established by Jesus's death on a cruel cross. Since God sent his Son here to die for us and make salvation possible, does it make sense to give less than the Jews were required to give under the old law? I think not. The verse quoted above from Mark 12 was a statement by Jesus telling about a widow who gave a couple of small coins, which was all that she had to live on. She could have given just one of her two coins. That would have been 50%, but she gave everything she had. Jesus also told the wealthy ruler in Luke 18:18 to sell everything that he owned and give it to the poor if he wanted to follow Him. Giving everything is a lot more than giving 10%. I don't think Jesus intended for us to give 100% of our money unless we love our money more than we do Him. He also taught us to cut off our hand or pluck out our eyes if they caused us to sin. The point is that He wants us to put Him first in our lives and not worship money or the things that it buys. In Matthew 6:24, He said that we cannot serve two masters. We cannot serve both God and money. Proverbs 11:28 says "He who trusts in his riches will fall, but the righteous shall flourish as the green leaf." I mention all of this to make my point that it is pretty clear in my mind that 10% is the minimum that we should give to God, and we should never put money or anything else ahead of God.

When our children were very young, I had a reasonably good job, but it was early in my career and money was always tight. I remember one time when a deacon came up to me after church and asked if I needed a loan. I was so embarrassed. The check that I wrote to the church the previous week had bounced because there was no money in our checking account. I apologized and assured him that I would replace the bad check with a good one. I suppose we gave more than we had that day (smile), but it all worked out and I learned a lesson.

I remember another time when we were living in St Louis and the children were teenagers. We were still struggling financially, like most people. We lived paycheck to paycheck, but somehow managed to get the bills paid. Even during this time, we gave generously to the church each week, but a missionary needed extra money and we were asked if we could help. We couldn't afford it but gave the money anyway. I figured we would find some way to pay the bills that month. I was surprised when we received an unexpected check a couple of weeks later that exceeded the amount that we had given to the missionary. That became a trend. It seemed like the more we tried to be generous in our giving, the more my pay increased at work. I heard a preacher say once that when it comes to giving, God has a bigger bucket than we do. We have a tiny pail that we use to make gifts to Him, but He has a huge barrel that He uses to make gifts to us. I truly believe that. We cannot outgive God. He always gives us far greater gifts than we can give Him, and I include money in that.

Today, my family is blessed beyond belief, including financially, and it all came from God. I don't think God blessed me with financial wealth because he wanted me to have the money. I think He gave it to me to share with others, and I try to do that. Think of the parable of the talents in Matthew 25:14-30. The servants who handled their lord's money wisely were given even more money. The servant who held on to what he was given and didn't do anything with it was punished severely.

I want to mention a couple of other important points on giving. The first is to pay God first. Don't give God the leftovers from your monthly income. Decide how much you are giving and don't decrease that if bills pile up. God will provide a way for you to cover the bills, and He doesn't want to be less important than your bills. Read Dave Ramsey's book Financial Peace or take one of the Financial Peace courses. He will teach you how to manage your money, get out of debt, and stop worrying about money. He will also teach you to reach the point where you can share your wealth with others.

Also, be generous with giving your time. Volunteer. Help other people who are less fortunate. Be alert and pay attention to others who may be hurting in some way. Help them if you can. Sometimes they need money, but often they just need you to do an act of kindness. Take food to them or offer an encouraging word. Many people just need someone to listen, and that requires a gift of your time. I am so proud of my immediate adult family members. All of them are great examples of giving time as well as money to help others.

Listen closely to those in need but be careful about giving advice. If you can, get them involved in working with you to help others. This changes their focus from internal (their own problems) to external (meeting the needs of other people) and provides them an opportunity to grow and be a servant like you.

Never forget that God will bless you far more than you will be able to bless others with your time and money ... no matter how hard you try or how much you give. God has a long arm.

▌REMEMBER:

- God says to test Him ... He will open the floodgates of heaven to reward generous givers.
- Pay God first.
- Be generous with both your money and your time.

CHAPTER 14

FORGIVE AND ACCEPT FORGIVENESS

The weak can never forgive. Forgiveness is the attribute of the strong.

– Mahatma Gandhi

When you forgive, you in no way change the past but you sure do change the future.

– Bernard Meltzer

If you forgive men their trespasses, your heavenly Father will also forgive you. But if you don't forgive men their trespasses neither will your Father forgive your trespasses. Matthew 6:14-15

Peter said to Him, "Lord, how often will my brother sin against me and I forgive him? Until 7 times?" Jesus said to him "I don't tell you until 7 times, but until 70 times 7." Matthew 18:21-22

If we say that we have no sin, we deceive ourselves and the truth is not in us. 1 John 1:8

I don't know how it happened, but I almost forgot to include this chapter on forgiveness. One of the main things that I have learned in my lifetime is that we all make mistakes and we all sin. We all need forgiveness from God, from our family, from our friends, and from many others in whom we come in contact. I have been blessed to receive such forgiveness and I pray that all who read this book will be able to enjoy that same blessing. Believe me, I have made whoppers of mistakes in my life so far and expect to continue doing so. None of us are perfect, especially not me. God has always used His long arm to rescue me, forgive me, and restore me.

The Bible is also full of people who made mistakes and recovered from them because they were forgiven but my favorite example is Peter. He was a bold man who made his living as a fisherman. He risked his life frequently by going out on the sea in a small boat that could easily be capsized in a sudden storm. He was also brave enough to walk away from that career to follow Jesus. Yet, as predicted, Peter denied Jesus three times just before Jesus was crucified. I know he felt miserable afterwards. How could he, Peter, have done such a thing? How could he ever recover from such a downfall as that? How could he live with himself? The answer is simple. Jesus forgave Peter.

A few days after Jesus was raised from the dead, he appeared to Peter and some of the other disciples. He asked Peter if he loved him. He asked him three times if he loved Him, and Peter said yes all three times, albeit using a different Greek word for love in each response except the last time. Jesus forgave Peter and gave him the honor of being the apostle chosen to deliver the famous gospel sermon on the day of Pentecost to launch the church. Jesus can and does forgive us when we make mistakes too.

As the Bible says, we must also forgive others, if we want Jesus to forgive us. We are all human and make mistakes. I do not expect perfection in others and I hope they do not expect perfection in me either. We need to forgive each other ... not just once or twice, but time after time (70 times 7). Do this even if someone does something that hurts you deeply. Find a way to forgive them instead of seeking revenge or harboring hatred or disdain for that person. Romans 12:18-20 says, "If it is possible, as far as it depends on you, live at peace with everyone. Do not take revenge, my dear friends, but leave room for God's wrath, for it is written: 'It is mine to avenge; I will repay,' says the Lord."

▌REMEMBER:

- No one is perfect
- Forgive others for their mistakes
- Keep on forgiving
- Don't just give people a second chance, but give them 70 times 7 chances
- Accept forgiveness for your mistakes
- Don't hold a grudge or take revenge, let God take care of that.

CHAPTER 15

KEEP THESE FINAL THOUGHTS IN YOUR HEART

For when the One Great Scorer comes to write against your name, He marks – not that you won or lost – but how you played the game.

– Grantland Rice,
American sportswriter

I expect to pass through life but once. If, therefore, there be any kindness I can show, or any good thing I can do to any fellow being, let me do it now, for I shall not pass this way again.

– William Penn

Trust in Yahweh (God), and do good. Dwell in the land and enjoy safe pasture. Psalms 37:3

Watch! Stand firm in the faith! Be courageous! Be strong! Let all that you do be done in love. 1 Corinthians 16:13-14

It is said that we are the architect of our own fate. In other words, the actions we take and the decisions we make today are building blocks that are used to construct our future. I know that each of you is different from the others, and you will all face different circumstances in life. Nevertheless, I pray that as you take actions and make those decisions that determine your future, you will trust in God and do good. You will make mistakes. None of us are perfect, but never forget that God's arm is not too short to guide you and protect you forever, regardless of circumstances.

Always keep the 23rd Psalm in mind as you live your life:

Yahweh (God) is my shepherd.
I shall lack nothing.
He makes me to lie down in green pastures.
He leads me beside still waters.
He restores my soul.
He guides me in paths of righteousness for His name's sake.
Even though I walk through the valley of the shadow of death, I will fear no evil, for You are with me.
Your rod and Your staff, they comfort me.
You prepare a table before me in the presence of my enemies.
You have anointed my head with oil.
My cup runs over.
Surely goodness and lovingkindness shall follow me all the days of my life
And I shall dwell in Yahweh's (God's) house forever.

Kenneth Bottoms, PhD

▌REMEMBER:

- God's arm is not too short
- All things are possible when you walk with Him
- Keep this in mind as you face daily challenges
- Choose to have a great life

CHAPTER 16

OTHER QUOTES AND WORDS OF WISDOM

Please thoughtfully read these additional quotes:

THOUGHTS FOR A LIFE WELL-LIVED

When you were born, you cried and the world rejoiced. Live your life so that when you die, the world cries and you rejoice. Author Unknown

You are the same today that you'll be five years from now except for two things; the people you meet and the books you read. Mac McMillan

I make all of the big decisions in my life by going into a cemetery and making the decision while I am there. Jack Swinehart, retired Navy chief, elder at Collingswood Church of Christ, good friend

The quality of a person's life is in direct proportion to their commitment to excellence, regardless of their chosen field of endeavor. Vince Lombardi, Legendary coach of the Green Bay Packers NFL football team

It's a funny thing about life; if you refuse to accept anything but the best, you very often get it. Somerset Maugham

Well done is better than well said. Ben Franklin

Honesty is the first chapter in the book of wisdom. Thomas Jefferson

There is no experience better for the heart than reaching down and lifting people up. John Andrew Holmer

He has achieved success who has lived well, laughed often and loved much. Bessie Anderson Stanley

We make a living by what we get, but we make a life by what we give. Norman MacEwan

Do not go where the path may lead; go instead where there is no path and leave a trail. Ralph Waldo Emerson

Happiness is an inside job. Author Unknown

Live as if you were to die tomorrow. Learn as if you were to live forever. Mahatma Gandhi

Learn from yesterday, live for today, hope for tomorrow. The important thing is not to stop questioning. Albert Einstein

Daddies don't just love their children every now and then, it's a love without end. Amen George Strait, singer

FAMILY SUCCESS

By all means marry; if you get a good wife, you'll become happy; if you get a bad one, you'll become a philosopher. Socrates, Famous philosopher

Love doesn't sit there like a stone, it has to be made, like bread; remade all the time, made new. Ursula K. Le Guin

Treasure the love you receive above all. It will survive long after your gold and good health have vanished. Og Mandino

When I was a boy of fourteen, my father was so ignorant I could hardly stand to have the old man around. But when I got to be twenty-one, I was astonished at how much he had learned in seven years. Mark Twain

Train up a child in the way he should go, and when he is old, he will not depart from it. Proverbs 22:6

Never, never, never give up. Winston Churchill

OVERCOMING OBSTACLES

I am only one but still I am one. I cannot do everything, but I can still do something. I will not refuse to do the something that I can do. Helen Keller, American author and first deaf and blind person to earn a BA degree

Courage is resistance to fear, mastery of fear, not absence of fear. Mark Twain, American humorist and author of Tom Sawyer books

What matters is not the size of the dog in the fight, but the size of the fight in the dog. Bear Bryant, legendary football coach at University of Alabama

Don't be afraid to take big steps. You can't cross a chasm in two small jumps. British Prime Minister David Lloyd George

In the middle of difficulty lies opportunity. Albert Einstein

Believe you can and you're halfway there. President Theodore Roosevelt

Nothing in life is to be feared; it is only to be understood. Now is the time to understand more so that we may fear less. Marie Curie, famous scientist and first woman to win the Nobel Prize

ETHICS/PRINCIPLES

In matters of style, swim with the current. In matters of principle, stand like a rock. Thomas Jefferson

If you don't stand for something you will fall for anything. Author Unknown

Eighteen holes of match play will teach you more about your foe than 18 years of dealing with him across a desk. Grantland Rice, American sportswriter

Golf gives you an insight into human nature, your own as well as your opponent's. Grantland Rice, American sportswriter

Its not hard to make decisions when you know what your values are. Roy Disney

GETTING ALONG WITH OTHERS

If you judge people, you have no time to love them. Mother Teresa

I will speak ill of no man and speak all the good I know of everybody. Ben Franklin, one of the US Founding Fathers

Don't carry a grudge. While you're carrying the grudge the other guy is out dancing. Buddy Hackett, comedian

A friend is a gift you give yourself. Robert Louis Stevenson, author

Always be a little kinder than necessary. James Barrie, Scottish novelist and playwright

No one can make you feel inferior without your consent. Eleanor Roosevelt, wife of President Roosevelt

Be who you are and say what you feel, because those that mind don't matter and those that matter don't mind. Dr. Seuss

Do what you feel in your heart to be right, for you'll be criticized anyway. Eleanor Roosevelt

As we express our gratitude, we must never forget that the highest appreciation is not to utter words but to live by them. President John F. Kennedy

CAREER SUCCESS

There is no elevator to success. You have to take the stairs. Author Unknown

You see things that are and say, "Why?" but I dream things that never were and say, "Why not?" George Bernard Shaw, famous playwright

Imagination is more important than knowledge. Albert Einstein

Nothing in the world can take the place of persistence. Talent will not; nothing is more common than unsuccessful men with talent. Genius will not; unrewarded genius is almost a proverb. Education will not; the world is full of educated failures. Persistence and determination alone are omnipotent. President Calvin Coolidge

Never, never, never give up. British Prime Minister Winston Churchill

Failure is success if we learn from it. Malcomb Forbes, publisher of Forbes magazine

Even if you're on the right track, you'll get run over is you just sit there. Will Rogers, famous humorist

I'm opposed to millionaires, but it would be dangerous to offer me the position. Mark Twain

Choose a job you love and you will never have to work a day in your life. Confucius, Chinese philosopher

The biggest mistake you can make is to believe that you work for someone else. Author Unknown

The woman who follows the crowd will usually go no further than the crowd. The woman who walks alone is likely to find herself in places no one has been before. Albert Einstein

Keep your eyes on the stars and your feet on the ground. President Theodore Roosevelt

We are what we repeatedly do. Excellence, then, is not an act, but a habit. Aristotle, Greek philosopher

If you work really hard and are kind, amazing things will happen. Conan O'Brien, television star

If you can keep your head when all about you are losing theirs ...
If you can wait and not be tired by waiting ...
If you can think - and not make thoughts your aim ...
If you can trust yourself when all men doubt you ...
Yours is the Earth and everything that's in it.
... from Rudyard Kipling's poem *If*

APPENDIX A

ADDITIONAL INSPIRING SCRIPTURES

Many are the afflictions of the righteous, but Yahweh (God) delivers him out of them all Psalms 34:19

Keep your heart with all diligence for out of it is the wellspring of life. Proverbs 4:23

Don't be afraid, for I am with you. Don't be dismayed, for I am your God. I will strengthen you. Yes, I will help you. Isaiah 41:10

... the mystery of God, both the Father and the Christ, in whom are all the treasures of wisdom and knowledge hidden. Colossians 2:2-3

As therefore you received Christ Jesus, the Lord, walk in Him, rooted and built up in Him, and established in the faith, even as you were taught, abounding in it in thanksgiving. Colossians 2:6-7

What does Yahweh (God) require of you, but to act justly, to love mercy, and to walk humbly with your God? Micah 6:8

My people are destroyed for lack of knowledge. Because you have rejected knowledge, I will also reject you. Hosea 4:6

... don't be anxious for your life, what you will eat, nor yet for your body, what you will wear. Life is more than food, and the body than clothing. Luke 12:22-23

Don't be anxious for tomorrow, for tomorrow will be anxious for itself. Each day's own evil is sufficient. Matthew 6:34

Trust in Him at all times. Psalms 62:8

For you are my lamp, Yahweh (God), You will lighten my darkness. 2 Samuel 22:29

Neither let us commit sexual immorality as some of them committed ... 1 Corinthians 10:8

Neither grumble as some of them grumbled ... 1 Corinthians 10:10

I have taught you in the way of wisdom. I have led you in paths of uprightness. When you go, your steps will not be hampered. When you run you will not stumble. Proverbs 4:11-12

... Choose you this day whom you will serve ... but as for me and my house, we will serve Yahweh (God). Joshua 24:15

Set your mind on things that are above, not on the things that are on the earth. Colossians 3:2

May Yahweh (God) bless you and keep you. Numbers 6:24

Let us consider how to provoke one another to love and good works. Hebrews 10:24

Children, obey your parents in the Lord ... Ephesians 6:1

Don't conform to the pattern of this world, but be transformed by the renewing of your mind, so that you may prove what is the good and acceptable and perfect will of God. Romans 12:2

... If any man serves, let it be as of the strength which God supplies, that in all things God may be glorified through Jesus Christ 1 Peter 4:11

Don't you know that your body is a temple of the Holy Spirit which is in you, which you have from God? You are not your own 1 Corinthians 6:19

Trust in Yahweh (God) with all your heart, and don't lean on your own understanding. In all your ways acknowledge Him and He will direct your paths. Proverbs 3:5-6

You are the light of the world. A city set on a hill can't be hidden. Neither do you light a lamp and put it under a bushel basket but on a stand and it shines to all who are in the house. Matthew 5:14-16

No one can serve two masters, for either he will hate the one, and love the other; or else he will hold to one and despise the other. You can't serve both God and Mammon (money). Matthew 6:24

For God so loved the world that He gave his one and only Son, that whoever believes in Him should not perish but have eternal life. John 3:16

Commit your way to Yahweh (God). Trust also in Him. Psalms 37:5

We know that all things work together for good for those who love God ... Romans 8:28

... whatever things are true, whatever things are honorable, whatever things are just, whatever things are pure, whatever things are lovely, whatever things are of good report; if there is any virtue, and if there is any praise, think about these things. Philippians 4:8

Man is born to (have) trouble as surely as sparks fly upward. Job 5:7

... resist the devil and he will flee from you. James 4:7

Yahweh (God) will keep you from all evil. He will keep your soul. Psalms 121:7

ABOUT THE AUTHOR

Kenneth Bottoms grew up in Kilgore, Texas in a loving and supportive Christian home with his mother and step-dad. He was baptized at age 12 in Rabbit creek, where he also went fishing from time to time as a child and stayed away from the snakes. As a teen and young man, he earned money at various jobs, but primarily by working as a golf course caddy and later as a roughneck on oilfield rigs. He used these earnings to pay for all of his college tuition and living expenses. He attended Kilgore Junior College and then Texas Tech University, where he received a BS in Electrical Engineering and met his future wife, Anne. A few months after graduation from Tech, he joined the Air Force and married Anne shortly thereafter. He served four years during the Vietnam War, was awarded a medal for his work on enhancing communications on the Worldwide Airborne Command Post aircraft which are in the air 24/7 and constantly available to launch attacks on enemies of the United States. He achieved the rank of Captain. He and Anne were blessed with two wonderful children who are now outstanding parents of four wonderful grandchildren. He met his birth dad for the first time over four decades after he was born. He also met his half-sister Pam and half-brother Harvey, along with their families. He was not aware of the existence of these siblings before meeting his birth dad. Pam is the one who searched for years for him and finally found him when he was working in St Louis. He served as a deacon at Churches of Christ in Dallas and St Louis. He served as an elder at the Collingswood Church of Christ near Philadelphia. His career took him to many cities and he retired from three different Fortune 500 companies, and is now living in Grand Prairie, Texas with his wife Anne. Over the years, he received graduate degrees and taught master's degree courses as an adjunct professor at Washington University in St Louis and at two prestigious universities in Philadelphia. He has never learned to stop working and now is a full-time volunteer helping incarcerated veterans through his church's prison ministry. He is also an advocate in Texas courts for children in the state foster care system.

04167984-00967800

Printed in the United States
By Bookmasters